My Giant Christmas Sticker & Activity Book

igloobooks

The Night Before Christmas

'Twas the night before Christmas, when all through the house,
Not a creature was stirring, not even a mouse.
The stockings were hung by the chimney with care,
In hopes that St Nicholas soon would be there.

The children were nestled all snug in their beds,
While visions of sugar-plums danced in their heads.
And Mamma in her 'kerchief and I in my cap,
Had just settled our brains for a long winter's nap.

When out on the lawn there arose such a clatter,
I sprang from the bed to see what was the matter.
Away to the window I flew like a flash,
Tore open the shutters and threw up the sash.

The moon on the breast of the new-fallen snow,
Gave the lustre of mid-day to objects below.
When, what to my wondering eyes should appear,
But a miniature sleigh and eight tiny reindeer.

With a little old driver, so lively and quick,
I knew in a moment, it must be St Nick.
More rapid than eagles his coursers they came,
And he whistled and shouted and called them by name!

"Now Dasher! Now Dancer! Now Prancer and Vixen!
On Comet! On Cupid! On Donner and Blitzen!
To the top of the porch! To the top of the wall!
Now dash away! Dash away! Dash away all!"

Can you find the missing stickers to complete this picture?

Whose Gift?

The children can't wait to open their presents. Can you find the correct stickers for each child, to see what Santa has brought them?

What would you like Santa to bring you for Christmas? Write your list here.

Dear Santa,
for Christmas I would love...

Santa's Snacks

Santa gets hungry when he delivers all the presents. Children usually leave food and drink out for him, but this time there's only a glass of milk.

Can you draw some mince pies, or other treats on the plate and add some carrots for the reindeer?

Which Way?

Help Santa deliver the gifts.
Find the missing reindeer sticker to complete the picture.
Which route leads Santa to the house with the little boy in?

a.

b.

c.

Reindeer Muddle

Look at the picture below of Dasher, Dancer, Prancer, Vixen, Comet, Cupid, Donder and Blitzen.

Circle the reindeer that appears twice.

a.

b.

c.

d.

e.

f.

g.

h.

Tree Decorations

Shade the Christmas tree using the Key provided. Using your stickers, place some gifts under the tree.

- blue
- green
- red
- yellow
- black
- brown

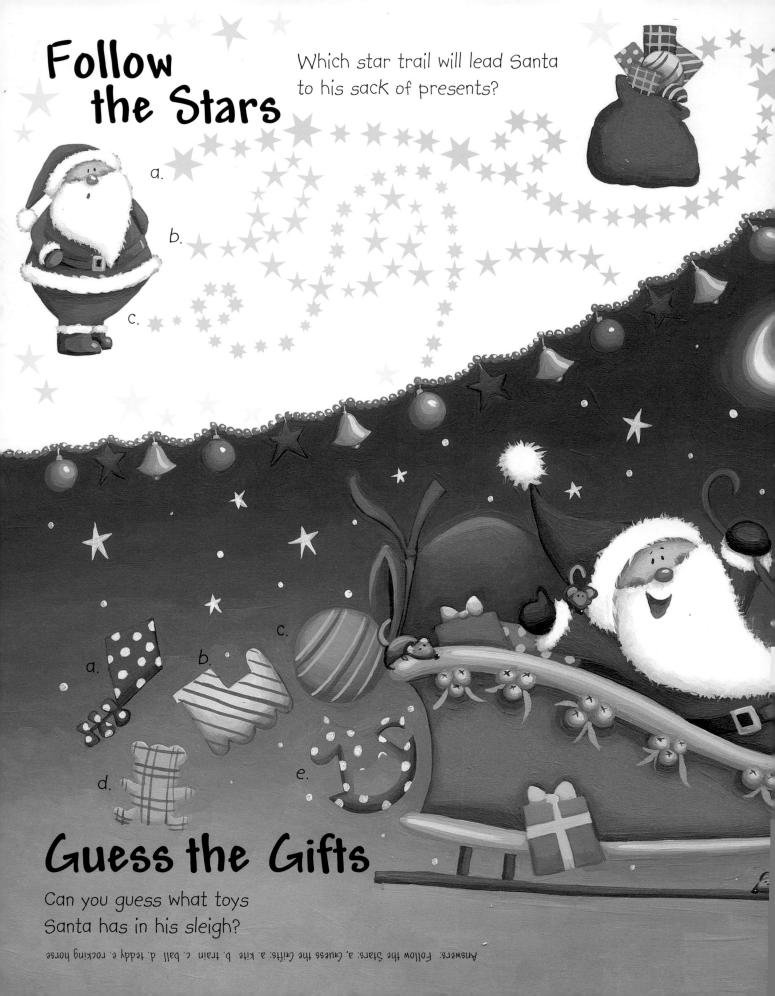

Follow the Stars

Which star trail will lead Santa to his sack of presents?

a.

b.

c.

Guess the Gifts

Can you guess what toys Santa has in his sleigh?

a.

b.

c.

d.

e.

Join the Dots

Join the bells to see who is pulling the sleigh.
Then decorate the picture.

Mischievous Mice

There are six mice hiding in this
picture. Can you spot them all?

Festive Fun

Help to get the house ready for Santa's arrival.
Use your stickers to hang up stockings by the
fireplace, leave gifts under the tree and add baubles
to the tree.

Santa's Sleigh

1. Fold the tab, on the picture of the presents, along the dotted line. Then push through the vertical slot on the picture of the sleigh, as shown in figure a.

2. Fold back the sleigh support, along the dotted line, so the sleigh stands up, as shown in figure b.

3. Push the locking tabs through the slots on the reindeer and fold back the leg supports, as shown in figure c.

4. Push the reigns on the sleigh through the slots on the reindeer, as shown, in figure d.

figure.a

figure.b

figure.c

figure.d

The Night Before Christmas

Which Way?

Festive Fun

locking
tabs

Christmas Cookies

Why not make some Christmas cookies to leave out for Santa?
Always ask a grown-up to help you when you are cooking.

Ingredients:

140g, 5oz, or 1 cup icing sugar, sieved
1 tsp vanilla extract
1 egg yolk
225g, 8oz, or 1 cup butter, cut into cubes
450g, 14 oz, or 3½ cups plain flour, sieved

To decorate:

250g, 10 oz, or 2 cups icing sugar, sieved
Edible gold and silver balls
Food dye

Equipment

A mixing bowl
A wooden spoon, or electric
hand mixer
2x baking trays
A wire rack
Star/Christmas tree cookie cutters
Cling film
Baking paper

Instructions:

1. Before you start, wash your hands.
2. Pre-heat the oven to 375°F, 190°C, or Gas Mark 5. Ask an adult to do this for you.
3. Line two baking trays with non-stick baking paper.
4. Put the icing sugar, vanilla extract, egg yolk and butter into a mixing bowl and beat together until the mixture is smooth.
5. Add the flour and mix to a firm dough.
6. Shape the dough into two flat discs and wrap in cling film. Put them into the refrigerator for 20 to 30 mins.
7. Roll the dough on a lightly-floured surface, until one finger thick.
8. Press out your Christmas shapes using your cutters.
9. Place on the baking trays and bake for 10 to 12 mins until lightly golden.
10. Put the cookies onto a wire rack to cool.
11. Mix the icing sugar with a few drops of cold water and food dye to make a thick, but still runny icing.
12. Spread the icing over the cooled biscuits and decorate with edible gold and silver balls.

Try not to eat them all before Santa gets to your house!

Find Dasher's Dinner

Help Dasher find his way through the maze to the food.

Handprint Santa Christmas Card

You will need:

Large pieces of card in bright shades
Washable water-based white paint
Washable water-based pink paint
Washable water-based red paint
Scissors (with adult supervision)
Paint brushes
Red paper
Glue
Googly eyes
A black pen

Instructions:

1. Fold your large piece of card in half to make a greetings card.

2. Cut a jacket shape out of red paper and stick onto the card, as shown.

3. Cut a Santa hat shape out of red paper. Stick the hat above the jacket, leaving a gap of about 5cm (2 inches).

4. Mix together some pink and white paint to make a light pink shade and paint a circle between the hat and the jacket. This is Santa's face.

Reindeer Food

5. Wait for the face to dry and then with a large paint brush, paint white paint directly onto the palm of your hand and your fingers.

6. Make a handprint on the front of your card. Your fingers should be facing down towards the bottom of the card. This will be Santa's beard. Now wash your hands!

to sam,

Happy Christmas

love from Jo xxx

7. Paint two pink circles for rosy cheeks onto Santa's face with a small paint brush. Paint one red circle for the nose and stick on two googly eyes.

8. Dip your little finger in white paint and press down each side of Santa's face. This is his hair.

9. Put white circles of paint along the edge of the hat for fur and one white circle for the hat's bobble.

Now write your message inside and send it to someone special.

What doesn't Belong?
Circle the things that don't belong at Christmas time.

a.
c.
e.
g.
i.
b.
d.
f.
h.
j.

Where's my Shadow?
Which shadow matches which reindeer
Draw a line between them

1.
b.
3.
a.
2.
c.

Santa Christmas Tree Decorations

You will need:

Red card
White card
Black paper
Cotton wool
Gold paper
Crayons, or felt-tip pens
Scissors (with adult supervision)
Craft glue
String, or ribbon

To make Santa

1. With the help of an adult, cut out a circle of white card, about 5cm (2in) across and draw Santa's face on to it. Don't forget his rosy cheeks.
2. Cut out a circle of red card, about 10cm (4in) across. Glue the white circle onto the top of the red circle, as shown.
3. Stick a thin strip of black paper across the red circle. This is Santa's belt.
4. Cut out a small square of gold paper to make the buckle and stick it in the middle of the belt.
5. Cut out a triangle hat-shape in red card and glue it on top of Santa's head.
6. Glue a small blob of cotton wool onto the end of the hat and more across the bottom edge.
7. Glue some cotton wool around Santa's face for a beard.
8. Punch a small hole in Santa's hat and thread through some string, or ribbon.

Now hang Santa on your Christmas tree. Why not make lots?

Santa's Sleigh

What a Mess!

It's been so busy that Santa's workshop has got into a bit of a mess! Can you help find the following things?

8 candy canes
A toy train
A rubber duck
4 teddy bears
Purple ribbon
3 mice

Match the Shadow

Match the elf with its correct shadow.

Reindeer Dinners

The reindeer were given ten carrots each for dinner.
Find the carrot stickers that match and then answer
the questions below.
Which hungry reindeer has eaten the most carrots?
Which reindeer has eaten fewest carrots?

Dot-to-Dot

Complete this dot-to-dot. Can you guess what toy it is?

Santa's Workshop

This elf is making toys in Santa's workshop. Help him put the right parts together by drawing lines to connect them.

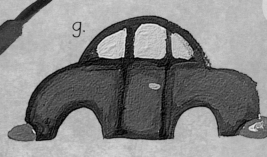

d.

g.

c.

h.

b.

f.

i.

e.

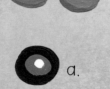

a.

Elf Pictures

Follow the instructions below and draw a picture of an elf. Then, stick on a photo of your own face, so it looks like you.

ADD YOUR
PHOTO HERE

1. Draw a body.

2. Add some arms and hands.

3. Add some legs and elf shoes.

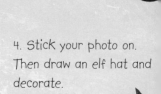

4. Stick your photo on. Then draw an elf hat and decorate.

Santa's Sleigh

The elves are making Santa a new sleigh. To see what it will look like, shade the sleigh using the key provided.

- red
- blue
- green
- yellow

Make Your Own Wrapping Paper

Make your own Christmas wrapping paper for those extra special presents.

You will need:

A roll of brown packing paper
A potato
Red and green paint
A knife
A pen

Instructions:

1. On a piece of paper, draw a simple star and christmas tree shape and with the help of an adult, cut them out. These will be your templates.
2. Cut the potato in half and press against a towel to dry it out.
3. Place the star template over one of the potato halves and use a pen to draw round it. Apply some light pressure so that the shape is visible after removing the template.
4. Now you can make your own stamp. Ask an adult to carve around the outside of the star shape, about 1/2 a centimetre (1/4 of an inch) deep, until only the raised star shape remains.
5. Repeat steps 3 and 4 with the Christmas tree shape.
6. Dip your star potato stamp into the red paint and dip the tree stamp into the green paint. Now stamp onto your brown paper to make it all Christmassy.

Festive Fun

Play this game with your friends.
Choose a Santa, or elf, sticker from
the book and stick it onto a coin.
This will be your playing piece.
You will also need a dice.
Take it in turns to roll the dice.
Then move around Santa's village.
The first person to reach the sleigh
is the winner.

START

1

2

3

4

13

14
Stop for a
mince pie.
Go back 1 space.

12

5

15

11

6
Help the elves
in the workshop.
Miss a go.

10

9
Stop to feed the
reindeer.
Go back
1 space.

7

8

Antler Antics

Oh dear, the reindeer are missing their antlers.
Draw them on to complete the picture.

22

23
Help to load the
presents onto
the sleigh.
Miss a go.

24

6

21

25

17

20

26

18
The reindeer
give you a ride.
Go forward
2 spaces.

19

FINISH

Sleigh Wash

Santa doesn't want his sleigh to be dirty on Christmas Eve. What do the elves need to clean Santa's sleigh for him?

a.

b.

c.

d.

e.

f.

g.

h.

i.

Origami Santa

Make this clever little origami Santa.

You will need:

A square of paper, red on one side and white on the other
A black pen

Step 1
Place your paper white side up and make crease lines, as shown.

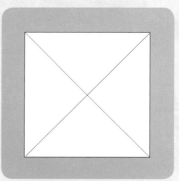

Step 2
Fold the corner in, as shown.

Step 7
Fold the top down again 1 cm (1/2 inch), as shown.

Step 8
Fold the corners back, as show[n]

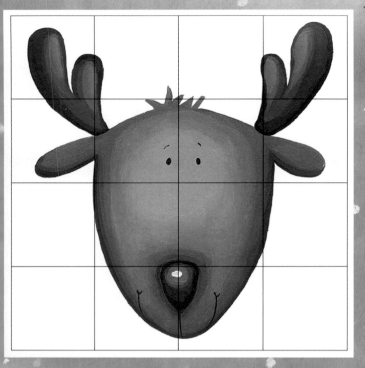

Draw a Reindeer

Use the grid to help you copy the reindeer.

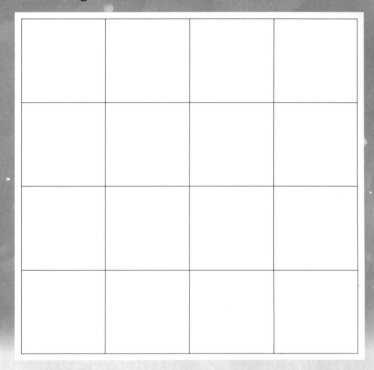

Step 3
Repeat with the other corner.

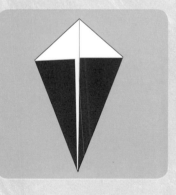

Step 4
Fold the bottom upwards, as shown.

Step 5
Turn over.

Step 6
Fold the top down, as shown.

Step 9
Draw on some eyes.

Step 10
Fold the top over to the right as shown.

Step 11.
Fold the bottom corners back so that it stands up.

How Many?

a. How many elves are in the picture?
b. How many of the elves have blue hats?
c. How many have bells on their shoes?
d. How many elves are wearing shorts?
e. How many have striped trousers?

Once you've answered the questions, add some elf stickers to give the elves some friends.

Rocking Horse

1. Fold the rocker along the fold lines, as shown in figure a.

2. Push the locking tab through the slot on the rocking horse, as shown in figure b.

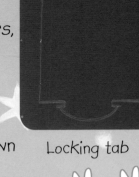

Locking tab

fig.a

fig.b

Standing Santa

Push the locking tab on the stand through the slot in Santa's belt.

Stand

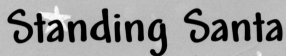

It's a Wrap!

Reindeer Dinners

How Many?

Reindeer Mask

Push out the mask, then push out the eye holes.
Fold back the tabs and stick them down,
Then, thread elastic through the holes and
tie a knot in each end.

Tab

Tab

It's a Wrap!

Follow the dotted lines to find the toy stickers that match the shape of the wrapped packages.

Bows and Ribbons

Can you help to wrap the gifts up nicely?
Draw bows and ribbons onto the gifts to make them look special.

The Twelve Days of Christmas

How Many?

In the Christmas song, how many of each thing is mentioned?
Fill in the missing numbers and find the missing stickers.

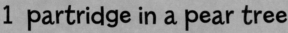

1 partridge in a pear tree

. . . turtle doves

3 french hens

4 calling birds

. . . gold rings

6 geese-a-laying

7 swans-a-swimming

. . . maids-a-milking

9 ladies dancing

. . . lords-a-leaping

11 pipers piping

12 drummers drumming

Moving Pictures

You will need:

A small circle of card

2 short pieces of string

A hole punch

Instructions:

step 1. Stick a sticker of a partridge onto one side of your card.

step 2. Turn over the card and stick a pear tree onto the other side, making sure the stickers are opposite ways up and in the centre.

step 3. Punch a hole in each side of the circle, as shown in the picture.

step 4. Now tie a small piece of string through each of the holes and tie a knot in the end.

step 5. Grab the ends of the string and twirl.

step 5

Now here's the magic part, it looks like the partridge is in the pear tree!

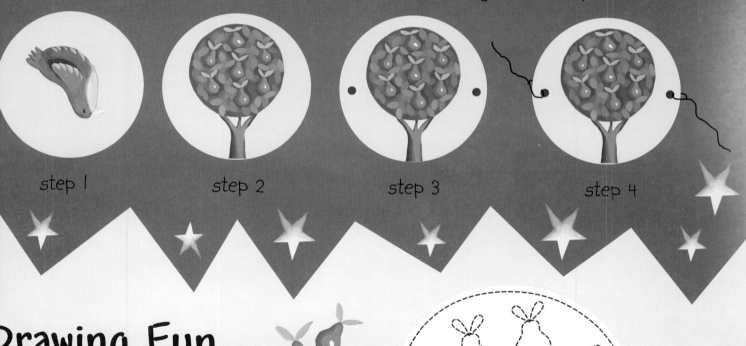

step 1   step 2   step 3   step 4

Drawing Fun

Draw a partridge in a pear tree by following the lines.

How many pears can you count in the tree?

Double Drummers

Can you shade the drummer to make him exactly the same as the other eleven?

Shake, Rattle and Roll

Can you say the names of the instruments below?
Have some fun trying to make the sound of each one.

a.

c.

d.

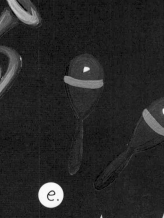

b.

e.

What's Missing?

Each of these pictures is missing something.
Find a sticker to complete each one.

Dancing Ladies

Make some beautfiul dancing ladies to hang up in your house at Christmas time.

You will need:

White card
Cotton thread
Scissors
A pencil

Instructions:

1. Trace the dancer onto card 9 times.
2. With the help of an adult, cut out your dancer shapes and make the holes where shown.
3. Thread the cotton through the holes on each dancer and line them up with their hands touching. Allow enough cotton at each end so you can hold it.
4. Decorate the 9 dancers in any way you wish.
5. You can now make all the dancers dance by gently pulling the cotton tight and waving the cotton. Or you can hang them up.

Find a Pair of Pipers

Which two pipers are exactly the same

a.　　b.　　c.　　d.　　e.　　f.

Leaping Lords

Join the dots to complete the picture.
Now count how many leaping lords there are.

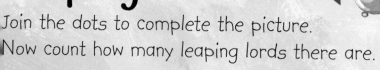

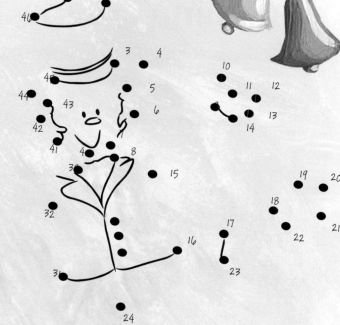

Swimming Swans

The seven swans are swimming through the reeds. Trace the path with your finger. Then draw along the dotted line with a pen or a pencil.

Odd Ones Out

Not all of the birds shown here are in the twelve days of Christmas song.
Can you spot the odd ones out?

d.

h.

j.

e.

b.

k.

i.

a.

f.

c.

l.

g.

Answers: Odd Ones Out: c, e, g, j, k, l

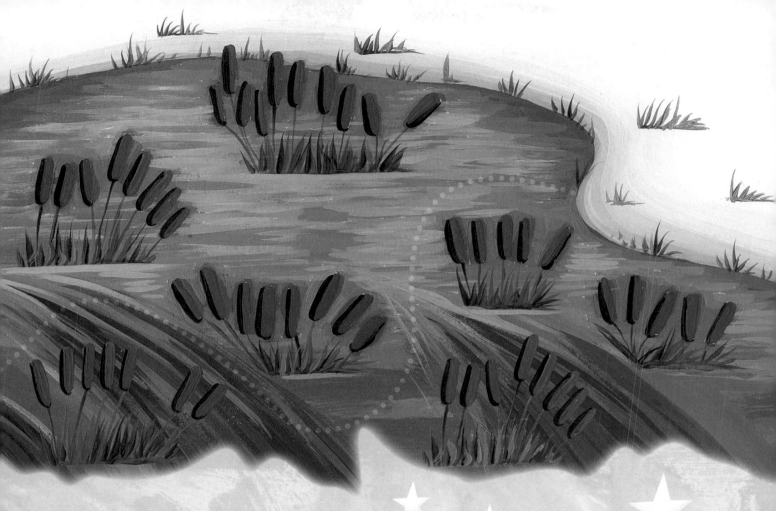

Down in the Dairy

The maids are about to start milking the cows.
Circle the things they will need.

b.

c.

d.

e.

f.

g.

Christmas Chase

Play this game with your friends.
Each player chooses a different sticker, from
the book and sticks it onto a coin. These will be
your counters and should be placed on the 'START'
star. Then take it in turns to roll the dice and
move round the board. The first to the parcel wins.

4 Stop to feed the calling birds. Go back 1 space.

5

3

START

2

1

22 Help the maids milk the cows. Go back 1 space.

21

23

24

25

26

27

29 Stop to collect the eggs. Miss a go.

28

31

32

30

Gold Rings

Each of these rings belongs to a matching pair.
Can you find the ring that doesn't match any of the others?
Match each ring to it's pair and there will be only one left.

Hidden Rings

There are 5 gold rings hidden on the tree in this picture. Can you spot them all?

Goosey, Goosey

Find the correct sticker to match the number of eggs each goose has laid.
Then count the eggs and see which goose has laid the most.

a.

b.

c.

d.

e.

f.

Dove Decorations

Make some turtle dove decorations to hang on your Christmas tree.

You will need:
White card
Thin ribbon, or cotton
Scissors
Felt-tip pens

Instructions:

1. Trace the turtle dove and its wings, as shown, onto your white card.

2. With the help of an adult, cut out your turtle dove and wing shape. Make the hole and a thin slit where shown.

3. Draw eyes on either side of the head with the felt-tip pen.

4. Fold the wings along the dotted lines and push through the slot in the body (**fig a**), then fold the wings back down again to lock the wings into place (**fig b**).

5. Slot some thin ribbon, or cotton through the hole. Tie it in a knot, or bow.

6. Decorate your turtle dove in any way you wish and hang on your tree.

fig a

fig b

What's Missing?

Can you spot what each hen is missing?

a.

b.

c.

Which Way Home?

The calling birds are singing to help their friend get back to the nest. Which route leads him there?

a.

b.

c.

Memory Test

Look at the picture below for a few minutes.
Then close the book and try to remember what was on the page.

Christmas Decorations

Tie a piece of thin string through the hole at the top of each decoration, as shown.
Then hang them on your tree.
See if you and your friends can find all twelve of them.

How Many?

Goosey, Goosey

what's Missing?

Chilly the Snowman

Winter Wonderland

Play this game with your friends.
Each player chooses a different sticker, from
the book and sticks it onto a coin. These will
be your counters and should be placed on the
'START' circle. Then take it in turns to roll the
dice and move round the board. The first to the
ice palace wins.

START

1

2

3

4

5

6

7
Your sledge is
going super fast.
Go forward
2 spaces.

8

9

10

11

12
You slip on
the ice.
Go back
2 spaces.

13

14

15

16

17
Stop to say
hi to Chilly.
Miss a go.

18

19

20

21

22

23

24

Ice Palace
FINISH

Snowflake Pairs

Which two snowflakes are the same?

a.

b.

c.

d.

e.

f.

g.

h.

i.

j.

k.

Chilly Fun

Complete Chilly by choosing nose, button, scarf and hat stickers. You could even draw your own snowman and decorate him with extra stickers

Safe Sledging

Chilly is sledging across the ice. Draw a line to help him get across the ice and back to his igloo without falling down the holes and cracks.

Chilly's Home

Draw a Sledge

These children can't join in with the sledge race until their sledge is finished!

Can you shade the childrens' sledge in for them? You can use whatever colour you like.

Skate Jumble

Chilly and the children want to go skating, but the skates have got mixed up in the cupboard.

Can you help find the five pairs? Draw lines to connect them.

a.
b.
c.
d.
e.
f.
g.
h.
i.
j.
k.
l.
m.
n.
o.
p.
q.
r.
s.

Coconut Snowballs

These are deliciously simple to make.

You will need

An ice cream scoop
Mini-muffin wrappers
Tray (for freezer)
Foil, or cling film

Ingredients

A tub of vanilla ice cream
A packet of desiccated coconut
A large bar of white chocolate (optional)

Instructions

1. Scoop out ice cream balls with a small ice cream scoop.
2. Then roll each ball in the desiccated coconut. Place them in paper mini-muffin wrappers on a tray.
3. Cover with foil, or cling film, and freeze.

Alternatively, you could ask an adult to help you melt some white chocolate. Quickly dip the ice cream ball in the melted chocolate before rolling it in the coconut and freezing.

Keeping Warm

It's important to dress up warmly when it's cold outside. Spot the clothing you wouldn't wear in winter and circle it.

Ice Maze

Chilly is going on an adventure to visit Santa Claus. Help him get through the icy maze to find Santa. Remember to avoid the polar bears.

Snowball Fight

Chilly and the children are throwing snowballs.
Who has the most snowballs, Chilly, or the children?
Draw some more snowballs onto the picture.

Keep Chilly Cool

Chilly likes to be really cold, otherwise he will melt.

Draw a ✔ through the cold things and a ✗ through the hot things.

a.

b.

c.

e.

f.

g.

h.

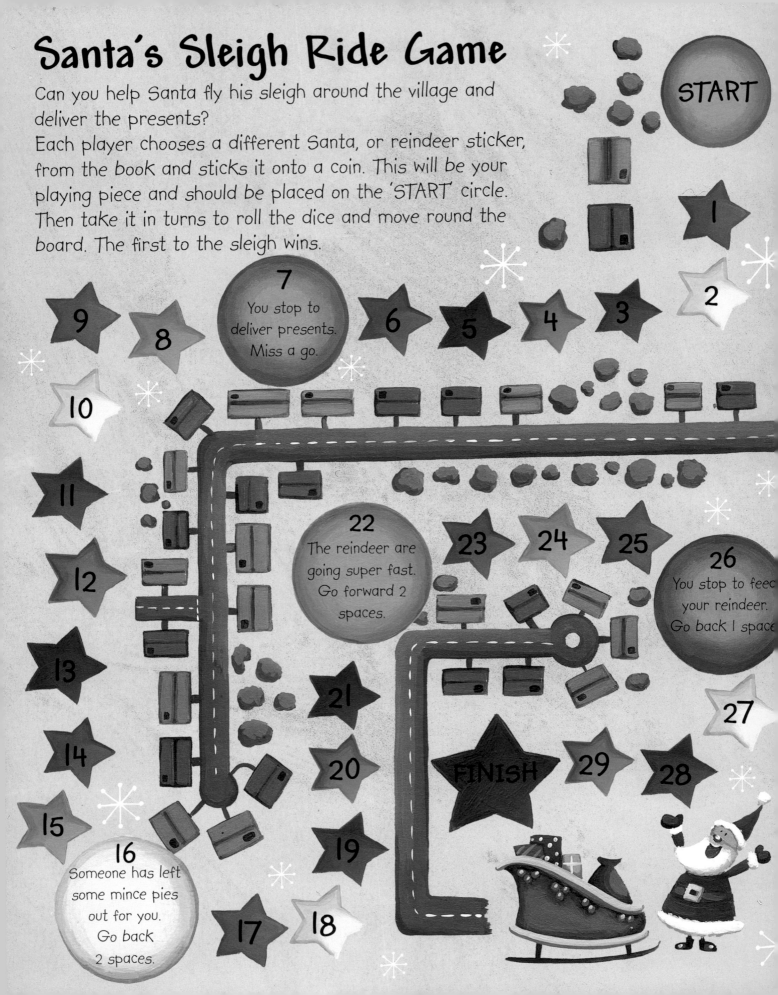